THE SILVER STAIR

the apocryphile press
BERKELEY, CA
www.apocryphile.org

apocryphile press
BERKELEY, CA

Apocryphile Press
1700 Shattuck Ave. #81
Berkeley, CA 94709
www.apocryphile.org

First published in London by Herbet & Daniel, 1912.
Apocryphile Press Edition, 2011.

Printed in the United States of America.
ISBN 978-1-937002-05-3

FORGAEL : *It is love that I am seeking for.*
But of a beautiful, unheard-of kind
That is not in the world.

AIBRIC : *And yet the world*
Has beautiful women to please every man.

FORGAEL : *But he that gets their love after the*
fashion
Loves in brief longing and deceiving hope
And bodily tenderness. . . .

AIBRIC : *All that ever loved*
Have loved that way—there is no other
way.

FORGAEL : *Yet never have two lovers kissed*
but they
Believed there was some other near at hand,
And almost wept because they could not
find it.

W. B. Yeats,—*The Shadowy Waters.*

(iii)

I

IF there be found, beside the Secret Name,
   One spell on earth effectual to cast out
   Moloch and Ashtoreth with all their rout,
One word that in my heart is as a flame
To burn up dull forgiveness and cold shame,
   One presence that hath compassed me about
   Too dear for pride of heaven or hell to
      flout,
Than love more ancient, more supreme than
      fame :

Thine only is it, thine indeed it is,
   Mother ; whose Sister of a like degree,
   Queen Mary, Mother of Eternity,
Hears God's voice shape that title still,
      whose sound,
Which now doth Zion as a rampart bound,
Smote once her heart with pain and shook
      with bliss.

II

YET by some path from that most hidden
     prime,
   Shut faster on us than His birth or death,
   God's feet came up toward us from Naza-
       reth,
Olivet, Tabor, Golgotha to climb :
Thence He in what joy's softness, sorrow's
     rime,
   Striveth with men, how hardly con-
       quereth !—
   This shall be told and borne upon whose
       breath,
Since in a cloud His own voice ceased from
       time ?

His ambush in a pebble's heart, His fleet
   Passage in light and shadow of leaves, O
       soul,
     Hast thou escaped ; wilt thou deny thy
         clay
   If thereupon He stablish His control
In mortal eyes that snare it, mortal feet
     That tread the windings of salvation's
       way ?

(vi)

CONTENTS

BOOK I

(vii)

CONTENTS

BOOK II

(viii)

CONTENTS

CONTENTS

(x)

CONTENTS

BOOK III

BOOK I

The predestined Lover, ignorant of Love, declares his Creed

SURELY this world is evil : Day and Night
    Offend us with an equal weariness,
  Being not strong to curse nor quick to bless,
But moving in a measured silence, light
And darkness. Also, who can tell aright
  Amid our dullness deepening to distress
  If aught be worth achievement ? or profess
That any hope is gracious in his sight ?

Therefore with equal eyes and steadfast heart
    Tread underfoot all excellent desire ;
      Seek no great thing, lest any hope or fear
      Lay hold on thee. So Death, when he draw near,
  Shall find thy soul not slothful to depart,
Nor without ease shall quench a little fire.

(3)

He questions his Fellows concerning Love

I HAVE gone up and down by many ways
　　To hear the voices of the sons of earth,
　To look upon their sorrow and their mirth;
And many have gone troubled all their days,
Yet with dry lips to one god render praise,
　　Holding his marvellous benediction worth
　　The utmost pang in which their souls gave
　　　birth
To changelings, that shall vanish at a gaze.

But of his might could no man tell me aught
Nor of the toil wherewith his grace is fraught,
　Whose presence is about us and above:
Yet if in very truth such god there be,
How shall he not reveal himself to me?
　O Love, O Love, exalt thyself, O Love!

III

He praises but fears Death

THERE is no god, nor has been, nor can be
  (Our folly this, and this our wisdom
   saith),
 Who is so strong and pitiful as Death.
Surely by ways innumerable shall he
Be summoned, and with high solemnity
  Pass on a tempest or a sleeper's breath :
  Call, and be sure he never loitereth,
Call, and behold he cometh unto thee.

Wilt thou desire him therefore ? O be wise,
  Turn backward o'er the trodden path thy
   face,
   And be afraid then to entreat him. Lo !
   This thing and this and that he needs
    must know,
  Who being parted from thee for a space
Around thy journeying hath set his spies.

IV

*He salutes those who have found
happiness in Love*

Joy, and the peace of sure and happy days,
    Love, and the wisdom of uncertain
      life,
  Faith, and the hope amid our evil rife,
Make strong your hearts, delectable your
    ways ;
Now that, above all chances and delays,
    Ye twain join hands, are husband now and
      wife,
    Even we who fear all things amid this
      strife
Dare in no wise discourage or dispraise.

Nor I the less salute you that no face
    Hath sent these heart-beats quicker, that
      no hand
      Hath e'er touched mine save in due
      courtesy.
Naught unto me Love yieldeth of his grace,
    Something to you, who make no small
      demand
      Of his goodwill : full may the answer be.

(6)

Again he questions others concerning Love

SPEAK, servitors of Love, speak, ye elect,
   Who hold your stations in his mys-
      teries,
  Tell us again how sweet the knowledge is !
And be not silent, ye who still affect,
Being ignorant, such wisdom, and expect
   Due audience ; for this last great gift is his,
   That on their brows who tread his palaces
Love's own sign flames, with his jewel are
     they decked.

Speak, for we listen : some hearts throb with
     prayer
   That they may do him service presently ;
Some scorn his hope and mock at his despair ;
   Some from his happiness would fain be free,
Nor any token of allegiance bear,
   For these things also end in vanity.

Of the mystery of God, and of the Divine Government

Either, as some old legend saith, He died ;
 Came down, and was incarnate and
  was slain,
 Then breaking from His bondage, once
  again
Took on Himself His majesty, His pride,
Leaving a memory of God crucified ;
 Or else He dwells apart in His disdain,
 Hearing the worlds cry out on Him in vain,
Till all things pass and He alone abide.

He giveth pleasure, but in pleasure fear :
 He giveth sorrow, but in sorrow doubt.
He fashioneth for us precious things and dear,
 But with destruction girdeth them about.
Sweet is His voice to call us—" Enter here "—
 And stalwart is His arm to thrust us out.

His appeal against the Poets

THAT ye, to whom all things of earth
    belong,
  Loveliness, wisdom, perilous renown,
  Whose minstrelsy is mighty to cast down
Kingship and tyrannies exceeding strong,
That ye, before your brethren and the throng,
  Should sing of love continually, to crown
  Life with its praise, albeit the high gods
    frown,—
This is not well, O Majesties of Song!

This thing we have against you, even we
  Who in your presence are not wont to
  speak.
For we have travelled over land and sea
  To find your temples : poor we are and
  weak.
  And where is now that joy we came to
  seek ?
What help for us in songs of love can be ?

VIII

He wakes upon a certain Morning

Dawn : and with dawn remembrance. Did not this,
This foreknown fear of memory and light,
Make harsh our else glad greeting of the
 night,
And trouble with expectancy its bliss ?
Now, ere our half-awakened eyes dismiss
 Their visions of the darkness, hath the
 might
 Of the full day put all our hopes to flight.
Dawn hath betrayed our spirits with a kiss.

One small thing wrought, one little thing
 forgot—
 Is there no other word of yesterday ?
For these shall pleasure and sustain me not.
 Naught ; or at most a lingering memory
 stirs
 Of laughing eyes and voices, and of hers
 Who parted from us at the turn of the
 way.

IX

Of the power of Love: of a Memory

To overthrow a nation for a whim,
    To ruin an ambition for a smile,
   Or, having walked with sin a little
    while,
To rival in high deeds the Seraphim ;
To shake the earth with exploit, through the
   dim
  Years to dwell secretly in a hidden isle ;
   O strange device of Satan ! O strange
    guile
And mystery of the craftful Elohim !

All breaking and all making of all laws
   Surely from one face hath looked forth on
    me,
    Who have not uttered nor my heart hath
    known
Desire of woman : surely Life withdraws
   Its burden from me while I walk alone,
  Silent, and musing on a memory.

Of the purpose of Cities

Towns have their wisdom: on the trading
    coast
  One is of pearl and one of dye-stuff proud ;
  Philosophy is in these halls avowed ;
These others hold command upon a host.
This little city of ours hath for boast
    As wise a knowledge ; wisely from the
    crowd
    Hidden in maze of silent streets and loud,
A deep fair secret, kept in the innermost.

How else so long have I gone up and down
Dull and in ignorance ? in so small town,
  So long have lighted not upon her ways ?
But now each street is a path venturous,
Each cross of roads a passage perilous
    With loveliness which is this city's praise.

He praises the diverse beauty of Women

FAIR women are the crown of loveliness
    Which hath of Life been throned and
       set on high;
  Unto a sweet and radiant sanctity
Their coming is a marvellous access.
They are the lifted hand of Time to bless,—
  His delicate word; soft vanities and shy
  Look from their eyes; their voices, passing
    by,
The very creed of Beauty do profess.

What shall be therefore said of others, they
  Who in a dark and shadowy order go?
    Indeed, these are the very crown of Life,
    Its minstrelsy in gardens, and in strife
  Its conquest: these all heights and sorrows
    show.
Theirs are proud eyes that have been closed
    on day.

XII

Of the purpose of Days

IF this be love I know not ; this I know :
  Eyes that have never cared for woman's
    face
  Seek now through every near and distant
    place,
Foolishly, if thy presence come or go,—
Heart that was proud of no pride is brought
  low,
  Losing all count of knowledge for a space,
  Nor is there found in hope or wisdom grace
Save through thee.   Also, I would have it so.

May many words or few declare it ?   See,
  At morn the day assumes her diadem,
    Some hope of thee ; all hours that said
      of love
  " What is it ? " hush themselves ; and,
    after them,
    If by good chance thou comest, high
      above,
The stars bear up the night for canopy.

(14)

XIII

He appoints Time and Place for Meeting with his Lady

THE threshold of my house thou shalt not
    cross,
  Nor shalt thou set thy foot within my door,
  As that or this man doth. I, being poor,
Amid my neighbours risk no treasure's loss ;
Light thoughts, light words, the most dear
    thing will toss
  Until it shatter on the earthen floor.
  And come not even when with three or four
I pace the gardens or by wall and fosse
Look in upon the town.   But rather thou
  Turn as I turn at sunset and pass through
Thy inner chambers toward those balconies
  Of prayer that God hath built for us.
    Things due
Shall there be paid and rendered, time allow
Content beyond all labour and all ease.

His Reconcilement with Life

WHAT of the Earth ?   That to the world
belongs
(I said) ; our cities gather in the dales :
What of the world ? No hope for men
avails
Over the number and pressure of their
wrongs.
I said : but now through sound of wrangling
throngs
I hear the thunder, hear the nightingales :
I hear the teller of all ancient tales
Whisper the singer of the oldest songs.

The world is great no longer, for the lands
Were wrought by God the Lord in tapestry,
And in His house hung round a single
room.
Where having entered, all unwittingly,
I half discern a dear face through the
gloom,
And in the silence stretch forth doubtful
hands.

His Profession of Love

THIS is the House and Convent of the
    Days :
  Hither all come. Certain have taken
    flight
  From vengeance, others are borne in from
    fight,
Others come tardily from merchant ways.
Also some few look and delight to praise
  God in tranquillity. All, with the rite
  Of dusk-time, to the company of Night
Make oath and are admitted. He who stays
  His journey here a little while shall see
  The whole dark Brotherhood pacing
    silently
Toward their monastic Chapel of the Past.
  Long since the Birth-tide ended. Who
    with me
Hath watched in abstinence through the
    Lenten fast
Hears now Love sing his Easter mass at last.

BOOK II

God has set the World in his Lady's Heart; the Lover questions of his Part therein

Out of her yet unmagicked eyes the light
    Drew, while as yet was neither when
      nor where
      Shaped for a glass to her : it was her
      hair
Out of whose darkness Day smote forth the
      night.
Her habit of wise deed in depth and height
    Hath bound Creation, measuring the air
    With Time and Distance : her august and
      rare
Necessities compel the lion and kite.

What thought in her—whose serene presence is
The world's epitome and genesis—
    Foreshadowed on the mind of God, awoke
The motion of my birth therein ?　What
      place
Holds that same thought now ?　Showed it
      in her face
    When yesterday she leaned to me and
      spoke ?

That the Love of a Woman is the Vice-Gerent of God

Night fell when toward this gated world
    I came,
  Nor there found peace—but light of
    shaken swords
  In battle of the crowd against their lords
And old men weeping for their homes
  aflame.
No general thought I saw nor common aim
Until there passed, amid the shouting
    hordes,
  With banners and the Provosts of the
    Wards,
A crowned queen. But I knew not of her
  name.

Then to my servants, my wise dreams, I
    cried :
  " Who is this Princess ? who this guard
    mail-shod ? "

And they : " Sir, these are captains of
    the world,
  Honour, Obedience, Thought ; their
    flags unfurled
Proclaim their mistress round them as they
    ride,
  Regent from the immovable throne of
    God."

XVIII

All Women bring him into Subjection to the One

H<small>ER</small> slender hands, that pluck at my
    ostent,
  Labour not solely ; they have great allies.
  Nor is her presence' war in single wise
Arrayed : unequal is our battlement.
Her embassies of beauty hath she sent
  Unto all women ; her they do avise,
  Assault on her behalf my careless eyes,
And wholly are to my destruction bent.

If there be thought that hath not seen, and
    dream
  That hath not lit on women, and delight
    That hath found nothing pleasurable in
      them,
And these be once opposed of Love, the
    gleam
  Of his least vassal's helm shall them
    affright
    With terror of their lady's diadem.

(24)

The Daily Ministers of Love

As by their chancellors or lords of state
    Kings and imperial rulers, each to
      each,
    Lend audience, as by hired tongues
      they beseech
Alliance, or threat war to loose their hate :
As priests, albeit in high things they translate
    Their sayings to the ancient language, teach
    The common people in the common speech
Wherein of secular matters they debate :

Let it be even so, that, when we greet,
    Courteous and cold, in any public square,
    The voices and the eyes which throng us
      there
May be ambassadors 'twixt thee and me !
Our souls are of too high a grace that we
Should always in our proper persons treat.

He praises his Lady with the Honour of Kings' Daughters

THERE are three women whose report is
    wide :
And theirs is for a blessed tribute brought
To be unto my lady, in my thought,
Music, whereat her own is magnified :
And first, God's Mother, when He lived and
    died,
    Who, being somewhile by Love's own
       passion sought,
    Was to His honourable triumph caught
(So far beyond me doth my lady bide) :
And then the winner of fair France from the
    hand
    Of England, and the breaker of defeat
(Because my lady's doings are a mark
To follow, as the comradeship of Arc) :
    Last (for the bearer of bitter things and
      sweet),
Helen ; by whom was ruin through Trojan
    land.

XXI

The Friends of the Bridegroom

For no escaping glances, words that fall,
   For no desire of soft lip or high brow,
  For none of these, beloved, do I vow
Love : somewhat yet is hidden in them all.
These are the echo to me, not the call ;
   A fair dream, whence is not full meaning
     now :
   However they be beautiful, and thou
Throned in them as a queen within her hall.

Rumour : the loves that once possessed my
    days
   Begin to whisper messages of thee.
They, while in conscious shame I stand at
    gaze
   Upon the frontiers of thy royalty,
Sound trumpets in thy heart's most secret
    ways
   And shake the portals unbeheld of me.

XXII

*That for Every Man a Woman
holds the Secret of Salvation*

Out of the secrets that He holds most dear
    (And these availed Prince Lucifer to
       quell,
    When, half heaven with him, from the
      stars he fell),
God bows the whole strength of creation
    near,
To breathe one, chosen, in the listening ear
    Of each man born, that he at last may tell
    In the great Judgement and be saved from
      hell.
This wisdom is forgotten in a year.

God, therefore, being merciful, takes earth :
    With hands of blessing and with terrible
      voice
    Each secrecy He fashions to a soul,
And seals it with His signet-ring of birth :
    Of which in credence shall a man rejoice,
      And in that hour his spirit be made
      whole.

XXIII

He invokes Love to Exalt Love

Love, who in cloud of changes earthward came,
　More mighty than all other powers that be,
　And learned in old arts of alchemy !
O Love, more wise than all men, whose dear
　　name
Through our fair hopes of heaven as a flame
　Lighteneth to the extreme of earth and
　　sea !
　Love, who hast sworn us of thy company
By vows of innocence and very shame !

Lift up our hearts within us, let thy foes
　Be smitten with the brightness of our days !
So they who whisper threats of divers woes
To come on thee, shall fail ; but we, O Love,
　Who follow thee down honourable ways,
Shall find thy favour and be glad thereof.

He desires to Suffer at the Hands of his Lady

BEFORE our hearts were sworn to brother-
    hood
  Didst thou not work against me a great
    thing ?
  For if these hours could to my knowledge
    bring
Some ancient treachery to be understood,
Some evil to make passionate much good,
  Then might my soul be called to pardon-
    ing ;
  Then might I gain, by that unequalling,
Place of equality near thee ; as I would.

Lady, confess ; that I too may forgive !
  Or hath indeed God left His gift of joy,
    Of peace, nor ever set His mystic guard
To keep it from all dangerous foes, that live—
    Ignorance, Custom—but to make hearts
      hard,
  This new simplicity but to destroy ?

The Desolation of her Absence

HER absence breaks the whole day's re-
    compense :
  Yet if so long I toil but for reward,
  And now at eve, coming to Time my lord,
He smite me on the mouth and drive me
    hence,
Shall I bemoan that sorrow and incense
  My soul against him ? or at heart record
  " Labour is vain if it be urgent toward
Pleasure, and love for payment an offence."

Look, if this day's loss were of this one day,
  It were a glad thing to have wrought so
    well,
And then be buffeted of pain away.
But now To-morrow lifts itself and peers
  For succour where no help is :—look and
    tell
How many morrows number how few years.

XXVI

Love the Precursor

All hours that Life had numbered and
    held fair
Shone on my road, as city lamps at night,
Against the threat of darkness, and still
    height,
And caverns where the foe might set his
    snare,
When suddenly thy coming shook the air,
    Thy presence rose upon me as a light
    Whereby I knew my way and came aright
Unto the house God chose me of His care.

I sojourned hitherto at certain inns :
    And now this house is strange to me, my
    bed
Is haunted all by clinging loveless sins.
I do attend a guest ; but who it is
    I know not, nor, when I shall hear his
    tread,
If I shall stab toward him or run and kiss.

Of those who have refused the Delights of Love

LET us remember times of famous men :
　　As, the old Stoics, learned lords and
　　　　proud,
　　Who sought not after Life with gifts,
　　　　nor bowed
Heads that his ringed hands might upraise
　　again ;
Or hermits, who in some dead wild brute's
　　den
　　Wrestled with princedoms, till the rocks
　　　　were loud
　　With spiritual strivings. These were
　　　　vowed
Alike, to scorn the sights of mortal ken.

Worshipful are the stars and joy and dole
　　For thy sake, lady.　This is understood
Little by him who never moans or sings.
But what wild vision dazzles his fierce soul
　　Whose testimony runs, that life is good,—
Who lays life by, in search for greater things ?

XXVIII

*That Love has in the World an
Enemy more to be feared than
Death*

THAT Death should ruin this thy house
    at last
No wise we held avoidable, sweet lord ;
Only, all danger else by us abhorred
Might we suppose was wholly overpast.
But now are every way thy treasures cast,
    Their warders being smitten with the
      sword,
The pillars whereupon the scribes record
Thy triumphs, shattered that were set so fast.

And he that wrought this evil shall amass
    Treasure, for he hath borne thee far from
      us ;
      And in some market, amid mules and
      spice,
      Shall jesting eunuchs buy thee, at a
      price,
To pour out wine before Tiberius,
Or serve the daughters of Herodias.

(34)

XXIX

Of Love's Enemies—Mammon

Nor diligent with priestly lips to warn
　　Hearts caught too soon with sense of
　　　earthly good,
Nor filled with love of holy maidenhood
(Albeit to us no children shall be born),
Beside the barns wherein we store their corn,
　　With robes unrent our rich possessors
　　　stood.
　　"Hardly," they cried, "ye can yourselves
　　　gain food;
Be cautious; live, as all must die, forlorn."

Therefore, because they have chidden us,
　　and we
　　Must crouch again to silence in our place,
　　　Hath God made answer, seeing our lips
　　　are dumb.
"Behold, for one sin, which is blasphemy,"
　　He saith, "against the Spirit, is no grace
　　　In this world, no, nor in the world to
　　　come."

XXX

He rebukes Fear of the World in Lovers

THAT man whose heart is moved by an
    eye's glance
And after by a lip's word is made great,
Who dare not then do battle with his fate,
Nor set his soul's life on a high advance
Against the times and years of circumstance,
    But is content in discontent to wait,
    Shall in a ruined house and desolate
Hear his last hope accomplice with mischance.

Contempt and length of life and bitterness
Shall be upon him ever : they shall press,
    With malice, through continual days and
      nights,
On all who for the broken years that be
Have pledged the riches of Eternity,
    Or gone about to marshal Love with lights.

Of Love's Enemies—Time

BECAUSE the passage of our great desire
　　Is as a wind that bloweth and is gone,
　　Because for each night's revel we put on
New crowns and robe ourselves in new attire,
Because the hot months break in flower and
　　　choir
　　Where last year such another summer
　　　shone,
　　Because the watchers of all flame heap on
Fresh fuel, lest in an hour they lose the fire :

Because these things are, though a man be
　　　wise
　　In pleasaunce, yea, be learned in its lore,
　　How shall he tell, by all grace gained
　　　before,
When at the last Change in his spirit dies ?
　　How shall he know, how shall his heart be
　　　sure
　　That even unto her his love endure ?

(37)

XXXII

He teaches the Love of Love

LET not the man that hath a little gazed
    On Love's good works be glad too
    easily.
  Surely Love will not with lip-service be
In any wise accredited or praised.
Nor his interpretation may be raised
    Beyond her office : his august decree
    Is but to letter forth his dignity,
Which they who reck not, fear and are
    amazed.

No voice nor hand nor eyes that men's eyes
    saw
Shall in their hearts eternalize Love's law.
  But they who serve their ladies, and adore
In them the visibility of Love,
    Shall loose their wills from change, from
    them no more
Shall his invisibility remove.

Of Love's Enemies——The Cross

In sight of stretched hands and tormented
    brows
  How should I dare to venture or to win
  Love ? how draw word from silence to
    begin
Tremulous utterance of the bridal vows ?
Or, as the letter of the law allows,
    If so I dared, how keep them without sin,
    While through our goings out and comings
      in
That Sorrow fronts the doorway of our
    house ?

It is the wont of lovers, who delight
    In time of shadows and in secrecy,
To linger under summer trees by night.
But on our lips the words fail, and our eyes
Look not to one another : a man dies
    In dusk of noon upon a barren tree.

He confesses the Singleness of Love's Deity

SERVICE is not in tears. Let Time and Space
  Usurp no god's prerogative, nor move
  Your hearts against the Person of this Love,
Who is not diverse : if ye see his face,
His is it, not another's ; in his race
  There is one goal. Howbeit, of old, the Dove
  That brushed your eyes and hovers there-above,
Kept in Gethsemane his hiding-place.

Bow yourselves, passing : There be other ways,
  Paths of ascent far other than ye know.
    Trouble not ; this hath he appointed you :
To understand his passion by his praise,
  To hear his whispers ; ye hereafter so
    May at his need succour the voice ye knew.

(40)

XXXV

" Thou, Child, shalt be called the Prophet of the Highest."

Lo now, a child : hear now the word, to
    all
Detractors Love's sole ultimate reply :
One of his light-armed troops, sent out to
    spy
About this land, and lure it to its fall.
Honey, whereof his soul may eat : clear call
    Of him immortal toward love like to die :
    Mark of our footstep toward him drawing
      nigh :
Steed of Immanuel, tethered in his stall.

Beyond all hierarchic Sounds and Lights
    These spirits look on Love's young In-
      nocency ;
That, smiting down on love through days
    and nights,
Struck forth the birth of Manhood recon-
    ciled ;
    Love smiting upon love in our degree,
What else should be for blessing but a child ?

(41)

Of Diffidence in Love

Yet sleeps she in her chamber : longer
    yet
  I at her soul's gate will maintain the guard,
  And watch beside shut casement, portals
    barred,
Till with the dawn her life its dreams forget.
Shall I dare sound then, lest the knocking fret
    Her thoughts, much weighed with house-
      hold service hard ?
    Or of the lit shrine break their still regard ?
I dare : against the door my hand is set.

O soul, knock loudly, nor too greatly fear,
  However thou seem miserable and poor :
    Estated by thine embassage art thou.
    It is not meet, for love's sake, thou
      shouldst bow
Too low.   O soul, knock softly, lest she hear ;
  Knock softly, lest her hands undo the door.

XXXVII

He is full of an Unknown Fear

WHAT swift and subtle fear hath power
      to blind
  My soul with hesitancy ? to bring feud
  Betwixt love's will and awful sanctitude
Till to be cruel is more than to be kind ?
In no strong net of utterance can I bind
    This armed fleet terror : thought it doth
      elude.
    Yet ever in my heart it is renewed,
And into civil discord taunts my mind.

All temporal swords of doubt that else had
    laid
    This soul waste as a wilderness hath Love
      Beaten with hammers into pruning-
      hooks
      To trim his gardens by life's pleasant
      brooks.
    There peace should dwell : there even as
      I move,
I hear the clash of arms and am afraid.

XXXVIII

That we know not yet what it is indeed to love

I LOVE her. O ! what other word could
   keep
In many tongues one clear immutable
  sound,
Having so many meanings ? It is bound,
First, to religion, signifying : " The steep
Whence I see God," translated into sleep
   It is : " Glad waking," into thought :
   " Fixed ground ;
   A measuring-rod," and for the body :
   " Found."
These know I, with one more, which is :
   " To weep."

Alas ! how oft this word rings through the
  port,
Where sailors of the further heavens resort,
   Where in this world their galleys ride.
   Few wot
Thereof its meaning ; they who dare trans-
  late
The saying into speech of man's estate
   Stammer upon the words : " I love her
   not."

(44)

His desire to conceal Love

I F I were with her I would keep her
    hands,
  And then we would not utter any word,
  But be so silent that there should be heard
The winds' far-off storm driving hours like
    sands.
There should be no more strife between
    commands
    Of hope or fear, till either was preferred.
    We would not think nor seek, but till one
      stirred
Dream with Time's self before his glowing
    brands.

But now I will not call her, lest there be
    God or some angel listening in the void
      By whom the sea shrinks and the stars
      are lit.
Would not our hearts choose rather—I and
    she—
    This same love were with vehemence
      destroyed,
      Than that a stranger should consider it ?

Of the Body

O HEIR of kingdoms, prince of destinies !
    Now are thy full years numbered to
      thee, now
    Dawns the sad proud hour when at last
      mayst thou
Assume possession of thy dignities.
The abdication of those regencies,
    Fancy and Learning, doth the crown allow,
    O fair and regal body, to thy brow
Of mortal and immortal mysteries.

These are the laws whereto thyself shalt
      swear,
    Ere thine accomplishment : To thine own
      use
    Thou shalt not turn the wide-brought
      revenues ;
    Shalt render tribute to thy suzerain,
God ; to thy brother, the lord soul, shalt
      spare
    All that he will, his loftiness to maintain.

The Body's Answer to the Promptings of Sense

" TREACHERY : Ah, my servants, with
      due show
Of honour will ye bring me forth the
    crown ?
Before my feet with loyal oaths lay down
Your staffs, your keys, your offices ? I know
Ye have sold my sceptre to the queen my foe,
    Betraying to her armies this high town.
    O slaves, go, tremble at your lady's frown,
Start at her smile : my purpose is not so.

" In secret audience I received from God
    The rule that I will keep—yea, I alone,—
      Even to the pulse-gates of this maiden
        tower.
      No train, nor strength of any allied
        power
Shall therein enter : sitting on the throne,
I, the lord body, sway my silver rod."

(47)

XLII

The Desire and Dread of the Soul

Come, for there is a garden that God made
    Before the rising of the moon and sun,
And not the great offence that hath
        undone
Life, till our years grow bitter and afraid
Of all things joyous—this sin hath not laid
    Denial on our feet, that they must shun
    Fair entrance. Come, beloved, there is
        none
Who shall forbid, none who shall dare
    upbraid.

(Hush ! also in a garden—O, too hard
The ways thereof that feet have trodden,
        scarred !
    Too crushed the grass by a prone agony !
But there, at night, by men with faces marred,
    Were olives gathered for Gethsemane,
    Was hewn the wood, shaped then for
        Calvary.)

(48)

To One, sitting at the Receipt of Custom, Love said, "Leave all and follow me"

A^N angel of the years stood up to mete
    The boundaries of the City, this side
    Youth
    And that side Wisdom, and the third
    way Truth
(Only the fourth wall yet is incomplete,
But loud at night with unseen workers' feet
    Who build up Death, without haste,
    without ruth).
    Then rang a great voice, shaking tower
    and booth,
The beggar's porch, and Love his own high
    seat.

Men say it thundered ; others, that there fell,
    Being falsely built, part of the city wall ;
And some few : " Therein God spake."
    Who can tell ?
But, for indeed this may be, if it be,
    O Lord of Love, assure me that thy call,
Thy summons, is not laid on me, not me !

Love said, "He that loveth his Life shall lose it"

I stood in Love's house, in the central
   hall :
About me wedded lovers moved and spake,
And all the odorous sweet air seemed to
   shake
With music : shone his victories on the wall,
Gained over heathen strife or market brawl.
   " Surely," I said, " none would this house
      forsake,
      Once found ; yet still there lacks a thing,
      to make
Perfect all joy that doth our hearts befall."

That hour a servant plucked me by the arm,
   And showed me near at hand a little door,
      Narrow, low-arched, and carven there-
         above :
      " Through me by losing shall a man find
         love."
      I tremble ere I open, yet am sure
That in his own house Love shall meet no
   harm.

(50)

The two Offerings of Love

CHOOSE now thy present for the king whose gate
    Shall ope before thee when thou com'st to die.
    Canst thou no treasure in Time's booth espy?
Casketed perfumes, scimitars of hate,
Dark wizard-hunchbacks, jewels, or graven plate?
    Naught of his goods this merchant may deny
    To them of the king's household: draw and buy
Good hearing with thy years of best estate.

But if thou choose love, wilt thou have this gift
    Fashioned in work of silver or of gold?—
Aureate, bought with toil and holy thrift,
With filling and with emptying horn and cruse?
    Argent, with tears, sad hours, and frustrate hold?—
Or wilt thou enter empty-handed? Choose.

Of Reasonable Persuasion

IF God, who fashioned earth and all live
  things,
  Commanded us : " Be fruitful ; multiply :
  Because We will not that mankind shall
    die,"
And gave life drink from His eternal springs :
If to our hearts the old desire still clings
  And timorousness but startle it more nigh,
  Shall we reject, under this mortal sky,
Fruition, whereof the night speaks, the day
  sings ?

If Love pass on toward governance and
  control
Not only through the dim halls of the soul
  But through these bodily courts majestical;
Tread with beneficent feet down alleys cool
  Of corporal pleasaunce, gardens spiritual,
In both shall we not honour him ?—Ah, fool !

He warns himself against all subtle Timidities

THE Adversary, coming to accuse,
    Heard the Lord laugh : " Yet wilt
      thou not adore ?
  Greatly thou hast not gathered hereto-
    fore,"
And spake : " Thou knowest me, whom still
    they use
To see clad round with evil, men refuse.
  But grant me change of raiment from thy
    store,
  And none shall seek thy blessings any
    more."
And the Lord answered from His glory :
  " Choose."

Then the Accuser took a crown of pride,
  A girdle of the praise of God to bind
  The hope of pleasure beyond mortal ken.
  All these he laid on one of his own kind ;
And with a staff of goodliness to guide
  His steps, Fear walked to drive Love out
    from men.

(53)

Of Renunciation

NEVER to seek her eyes with mine, to touch
  Never, with communing of joy or fear
  Her yielding hands of presence ; but, so dear
As needs is all her beauty, by so much
To hold it alien from me, think it such
  As should dismay the lover who draws near
  To his pale mistress on her flower-strewn bier,
Such as no strong arm, no loose hand can clutch.

It may be that a little memory
  Of meetings and of partings shall be kept
    Amid more great remembrance in her heart.
This is a secret thing : but as for me,
  There shall be lost no thought of her, except
    All love of God and of this world depart.

Of the Alternative Choice

KEEP counsel.   If thy blood plot with thy
    heart
  To dispossess thy royalty of will,
  Let no such murmur of rebellion fill
The mental house where Honour sits apart.
Ere thy desires be gathered, let none start
    Toward Thought, lest he be moved and
    quick to kill.
    In curtained chambers let him sleep, until
The appointed hour speed the mortal dart.

Then seize that house and measure it, the
    walls,
    The depth and height thereof ;   thou
    shalt not find
One hidden chamber.   Thine are its least
    halls.
    Eat, drink, be glad, and rise up, having
    dined,
To look on pleasant things ;   nor, when night
    falls,
    Wake, though lament be driven on the
    wind.

L

*The Lover will choose locusts & wild
honey rather than Dead Sea fruit*

SHALL this be all ? shall the song-maker
    spend
    Time and long toil and care, that we may
      turn
    From the wrought verse with hearts and
      eyes that burn
To see the moving hands, the neck's smooth
    bend ?
Yea, is this all ? for this shall all men send
    Thanks to the singer, that they may
      discern
    The wondrous head, the body's grace, and
      learn
More of its beauty,—till God make an end ?

Break we the lute ! though long we have
    delayed—
    Rend we the verse !—he shall redeem us
      yet.
    Destroy, destroy these chambers where are
      met,
Laughter, desire, and music of our sin ;
That amid ruin our violent hands have made
One may stand preaching, clad in camel-skin !

(56)

He demands of Love what is in truth its final satisfaction

L IGHTNING of heaven or torch of earth or fire
  Out of deep hells, and which indeed is
    thine ?
The stars that on December evenings shine
On frozen lands and waters ? or the pyre
Heavenward flaming, where whom nuptials
    'tire
  Are bound and laid by service-hours
    divine ?
  Or the red horror, the eternal sign,
Where they dwell who accomplish their desire?

Yet they who walk in starlight shrink with
    cold,
Desiring warmth ; and they who dare be
    bold
  To sacrifice, endure, if but a night.
But those whom Hell hath swallowed have
    no hope,
They burn for ever.   Other men must grope
  In darkness, having never seen the light.

(57)

Of the Attainments of Love

THIS is the end of love : the years that
    bring
  Passion with strength of living and its
    pride,
  Bring also grief, dull pain that shall abide,
And desolation past imagining.
This is the end of love : no fearful thing
  Twain that are one together shall divide,
  Nor, as the long years draw to eventide,
Shall their lives faint for any happening.

Is there none other end ? yea, one there is.
  Before Love's mazed, stricken, and hal-
    lowed eyes,
  In earth, in heaven gleam bright virgin-
    ities.
    To whoso is by terror at heart thereof
Or hunger of soul toward doom he knew not
    his
    Urged beyond hope, this is the end of
    love.

LIII

Of the Approach to God

If thou couldst rend asunder heaven,
    lay bare
  The uttermost foundations of the deep,
  Or if thy spirit could go forth in sleep,
Wouldst thou find out His city anywhere ?
Lo ! in eternity thou shouldst not snare
    His going ; there His court He doth not
    keep,
    Who hardly shall be found of them that
    weep,
Nor easily laid hold upon by prayer.

Thine eyes have seen, thy hands have touched
    the gate.
    Pass, for by love God sitteth girt about,
      And through love to Him shalt thou
      enter in.
      Yet, if thou mayst dare greatly and not
      sin,
Better it were to cry aloud and wait,
    Until He join thee secretly without.

The Lover prays to know God's Will

Lord Love, by thy keen fervency, which
    lit
On her of God, surnamed Immaculate,
And by the coming in of thy estate
Usward, and by thy harrowing of the Pit,
Though I be weak, and of a feeble wit,
    And though my heart be light enough in
      weight,
    I have a prayer to thee : think at what rate
Thou hold'st me, not I thee, to answer it.

O obscure Love, I will demand of thee,
    To know where thou abiding labourest still
      Both toward my lady and on her behoof.
Of alien journeys which is doomed to me ?
    Indeed I know not what may be her will,
      If I should seek her or should stand aloof.

He prays to know his Lady's Will

ATTEND upon me, Love, whither we
    twain go.
  Follow, my ruler, humbly as my slave
  Compelled beneath thine own imperial
    stave
To such obedience, whither we may show
All question to my lady. Bend we low
  Our heads at entrance; let the servants
    lave
  Dust from our sandalled feet. Naught
    now shall save
Thy purpose from her will, O thou my foe!
I am prouder here than thou art and more
    wise.
  Speak when she cometh, Slave: " Lady,
    my lord
    Here hath confessed his love and in
    these rhymes
    Lays at thy feet the governance of his
    times.
O mastery of men! wilt thou despise
  The bondage of the gold or silver cord? "

(61)

Of the high Comradeship of Love

Look up, the heavens grow ardent to our
    gaze ;
  Look down, the hells are rampant at our
    feet.
  And think ye here where such dominions
    meet,
The fires of your night bivouac can blaze ?
The shouting squadrons by a thousand ways
    Rend your pavilioned camp : their charges
    beat
  Your piled arms underfoot, or in retreat
Trample the tents that with much toil ye
    raise.

If I might gird her for the strife, set on
  —I, even a man, to this thing sanctified—
    Her helmet, and God's anger not be
    moved !
    O my beloved, if in armour proved
We twain might follow where Immanuel
    shone,
    Triumphant and to triumph, side by side !

(62)

LVII

Of Sacrifices lightly made for Love

It is recorded of queens' majesties,
    Certain among them loved, and for
        that cause
Put by their rule and maintenance of laws
With poor esquires to prove the truth Love
    sees.
Nuns also have been bold to turn back keys
    On evenings that ere troth-plight gave
        them pause,
    Have fled from convents, and with God's
        applause
Vowed their lives' fealty to Love's less decrees.

But yet I dreamed a greater thing of thee,
    Which if in difficult words I should confess
    No doubt but it should seem a foolishness ;
        No doubt but lovers' laughter should
        awake
If among men and women it might be
        That any had put off love for love's sake.

LVIII

Of Womanhood—the Citadel of Life

Life built the city of my soul, the mart,
  Towers, and quiet places of the dead,
And set Love there for Viceroy in his stead
With equal sway and of his powers great part.
But he himself in regions of thy heart
  Dwells, with magnificence : therein are spread
  His banners ; at his table there are fed
Times fugitive from Wisdom and from Art.

So, when white standards of a new host shone
About us, soon they took me and passed on.
  And now about thy gates the noise of strife
Goes up, yet how shall this thy City fall ?
  Seeing what futures throng thy streets, how Life
Directs his battle from the unbreached wall.

That the end of Love is clear only in the Light of the Soul

Love, gone a-wandering through this
    world of man,
  Through the wide mazes and the depths
    that make
The earth, man's body, knew not how to take
Such path as to his tryst directly ran,
Nor could find guidance, that the shadows 'gan
  Trouble his soul, until the stars that wake
  Movement in man, his thoughts and wis-
    dom, spake
Hope, and led through the hard roads'
  complex plan.

Yet so the way he saw not by their light,
  Nor robbers' haunt, nor lair of couchèd
    beast ;
Until the moon, the very soul of Night,
Shone ; then about all heaven there went
    the fame
  Of God, a message heard beyond the East ;
And to his high tryst Love at daybreak came.

Of the Answer of his Lady

THE praise of Michael : star to star hath
sung
 Far flying battles through heaven's firma-
  ment.
 The praise of Raphael : crowned pre-
  eminent
In lore of worlds and times and each new
 tongue.
Of Gabriel : while his feet one moment clung
 To earth, he with veiled eyes and proud
  head bent
 Received the holy-syllabled assent,
Whereon the loves of all the nations hung.

O if there be one secret path wherein
Michael hath clashed not, nor the Lord of
 sin,
 Nor any roar of any world gone by,
There, through this earth-night's hush,
 Prince Gabriel,
Set my confirmèd feet ; there let us tell
 Our tales of Love's most loving, thou and I.

LXI

Of the Paths and Times of the World

WHAT song hath any road except it be
    Of men and towns, of lights and
      fires that glow ?
  Nor any street, wherethough strong tem-
    pests blow,
Is not bound in by shut doors' mystery.
But how straight these paths, but how nar-
    rowly
  The most broad ways of this our city show,
  None other heart but hers and mine can
    know,
Nor ever any dwellers else shall see.

Cold roads of winter and green roads of spring
Are not more wide than twain loves' hand-
    locking,
  Each doubled way meet for a doubled boon.
For lonelier feet, more clear and sheer than this,
One bright bridge spans the dark of Time's
    abyss,
  One single silver gleam beneath the moon.

The Pain of the Slaying of Corporeal Love

Draw near, Beloved, let us crown our
    lord.
  Wherewith ? With jewelled circlet or
    with thorn ;
  Let him by knees as in his praise or scorn
Bent, be with honour or reproach adored.
Let chain of gold or malefactor's cord
    Bind round the mortal purple he hath
    worn :
    Let him with outcry to his throne be
    borne ;
For him be wine or vinegar outpoured.

God is he : hearken ! this accusing tale
Shall for his pain and ending best avail,
  In whose death-filmed eye breaks Deity.
Man is he : think not any thrusting spine
Shall less be sharp for power supposed divine,
  Or present darkness less for light to be.

*The Lover asks why he should
assume the Yoke of difficult Service*

"WHY stand'st thou idle?" Sir, no man
this day
Hath hired me to his service. "Go with me:
Join there my gardeners, labour diligently;
And what is right shalt thou receive for pay."
Whom will these vineyards profit, brothers? yea,
What guests, what friends with wine there-
from shall he,
Our master, feast through evenings yet to be,
Nor call to mind us he hath sent away?

Ah, envious soul! How know'st thou,
husbandman,
After the warred destruction of what
powers,
The breaking what hushed evils with a cry,
Those star and sun bound princes shall
draw nigh?
Or wouldst thou rather, through the idle
hours,
Lean in the market, as when the day began?

He disdains the Judgements of the World

IN this we are not careful to be wise ;
 Yea, almost men shall reckon us for fools,
Who, burdening their lives with heavy rules,
Can lift not up to heaven exultant eyes.
They shall keep watch if discontents arise
 Between us, whispering that our passion
  cools ;
 Save where, perchance, some follower of
  the schools
Muses above old parchments of surmise.

How shall he dare whose dull life hath not
  known
 One moment of the least of Love's least
  hours
  Praise, or defend us with ignoble pleas ?
Or they who, measuring all hope with their
  own,
 Make deaf our ears with noise of temporal
  powers—
  Beloved, what have we to do with these ?

His fear of Days to Come

BELOVED, ere we die we shall wax old :
  Shall not then even thy praise which
      now is sung
    About my spirit, we being proud and
        young,
Seem but the boast of poor souls overbold ?
Then shall we know that Love escaped our
      hold
    When from our days the shows of Love
        we flung ?
    For that no man may speak with alien
        tongue
The tale which only is in nature told.

Terror hath breathed upon me from that hour,
    Lest then, because our bodies once were
        lamed
      Of their own will, albeit by innocence,
      Death come upon them suddenly, and
          thence
Compel us toward his house of sorrowful power,
    And mock us while we stand beneath him,
        shamed.

LXVI

Of the Place of Abiding

UPON a day we issued, thou and I,
  Out of the gate of Time's regality,
Whose wharves run down to a tempestuous
    sea,
And to the borders of his realm drew nigh.
But there his knights who watch lest any fly
  His marches, strove, if we perchance
      might be
  Borne captives to their suzerain ; but we
Met them and overthrew them and passed by.

Then we rode on into the land of Love,
  By many royal citadels, and came
Unto the strength and capital thereof.
Herein is joy for all our hardihood,
  Joy that is told not of in common fame,
Nor is by Love's provincials understood.

BOOK III

An Ascription

" AND we believe in God the Holy Ghost,
    Giver and Lord of Life," Whose will
        hath rent
    The temples of His own accomplish-
        ment,
Rebuilding them to make of Him their boast.
The countless generations of our host
    Move at His bidding ; and in His descent
    Glows all soft passion, laughs all sweet
        content.
Silently serve Him they that serve Him most.

All lives of lovers are His song of love,
    Now low and soft and holy as a kiss,
        Now high and clear and holy as a star.
Slave in Man's house, yet builder-up thereof,
    The silver and the golden stairs are His,
        The altar His—yea, His the lupanar.

The Knight-errantry of Love

WHITHER so swiftly ridest thou, sir knight?
   "To my full halls where men hold
     revelry."
But whose is all this goodly company?
"Elect are they, the champions of my
     might."
How may we know thee, naming thee aright?
   "Love am I called and all men follow me."
What shall we have if we ride after thee?
"Health and fulfilment of thy lips' delight."

What is thy crest, sir knight, and what thy
     name?
   "My crest is Loneliness: my name is
     Love."
Ridest thou with no brotherhood of fame?
   "God and my soul and all the stars above."
Shall we find aught in following thee but
     shame?
   "Strange and familiar things and joy
     thereof."

The Lover praises Virginity under the Name of Artemis

HERE, on the height of highest mountains, here
  Far from poured perfumes, dances, and
    the shows
  Wherewith the city hallows whom it knows,
Love's ruler, Aphrodite, we uprear
In reverent honour, in a little fear,
    Altars to her whose following we chose,
    The goddess of the moon and of the snows,
The mistress of the bow and hunting-spear.

No care hath she for corn or clambering vine
    Or reaping-hours or busy sound of mills :
And hers the cottage is not, nor the kine.
Hands clear from touch and lips from any
     kiss
    Hail her beneath the stars, upon the hills,
Vestal and Queen, celestial Artemis !

He endures Loneliness

WHEN all the comfortable lamps are lit,
And all the windows shut upon dark
skies,
When no one any more is proud or wise
Or envious or clever with keen wit,
When unremembered the still moments flit
And pleasantly the changeful music dies,
When love looks out of dear familiar eyes
And a man's heart hath rest because of it :

We by the solitary paths descend,
Unheard, along the silent streets we pass,
See the lights shining through the cur-
tained glass,
And hesitate before the house of birth.
Here are content and laughter and a friend,
Voices of lovers, little children's mirth.

He endures Temptation

KING SCHOENUS' daughter, Atalanta, wise,
    Dangerous as the North Wind, who
      outran
On virgin sandals the quick love of man,
And watched the sword-doom with sword-
    cruel eyes,
Slacked not her feet nor did in thought
    despise
    Her loftiness, well-warded for a span,
    Yet held at heart of no more high worth
      than
Gold balls which for Milanion gained the
    prize.

What if, when else thou couldst outstrip, O soul,
    Thy eager and swift body, nor wouldst go
      Softly for that love's sake thou hast
      denied,
What if thou turn thyself and lose the goal
    For gain of smooth slight pleasures ?
      Here is woe,
      To run awhile and stay and look aside.

LXXII

He beholds the Dwelling of Love,
which many great Lovers desired
to see and were not able

Love hath his own peculiar courts, his
    halls
  And spreading gardens, girt by seven
    towers,
  And sentinelled by all the virgin powers,
His only freedmen, others are his thralls.
Around them lies the city ; trumpet-calls
    Not often sound there, but through
      pleasant bowers
  Lute music echoes, joyous are the hours,
The River of Life flows round about its walls.

Without are lepers and all evil things :
Within are wise men, warriors, and kings,
  Who mid their joys grow eager to assail
The silent gardens of the brooding Dove ;
  Over the central towers to prevail,
To storm the very dwelling-place of Love.

(80)

The Passion of Love.—1. Our Lady the Virgin

QUEEN, in a distant and forgotten land,
    Upon the borders of that harboured
        sea
Where glows the Beatific Mystery,
Thy builded palaces of silver stand :
And fain are all who see them to demand
    In holy fear and mighty love toward thee
    That they may follow thy virginity,
Nor lose their hope by any woman's hand.

But we, for whom no gladness shall restore
Past things, may enter in those courts no more,
    However pleasant be their shade and cool :
Who, while the stars on their white pillars
        shine,
    Dream only, listening by an orchard pool,
Of a dear face, too amorous for thine.

The Passion of Love.—2. The Lover hears of her in the Place of the Slaying of Love

IN many places had we sought for her ;
    That by her grace we might entreat the
        Son
For all foul evils thought of him and done,
Whose praise men told us in the days that
    were.
The priests that in her service minister,
    The messengers that on her errands run,
    Knew not her biding-place ; nor any one
Of those whom she to honour doth prefer.

We asked of peasants, but they mocked our
        speech ;
    Of kings, but they had made themselves a
        law ;
    Of sages, but they bade our hearts be still.
We did the hucksters of the town beseech :
    " One such as ye desire," quoth they, " we
        saw
      But now, with other women, on a hill."

LXXV

The Passion of Love.—3. Love's Present Agony

Anguish of soul : bound in each bruisèd
    limb
And manacled by tired feet, Love must go
Unto the Pavement, must with curse and
    blow
Be pressed by the fear-ridden Sanhedrim.
Then from fierce hands and hate and faces
    grim
    Shall he be barred by soldiery, that know
    Naught but his name, with ordered spear-
       shafts. Lo,
Hard on one side, the devil, tempting him !

Anguish of body : bared to popular eyes
    And popular lips that mouth it and are fed ;
Last brute deforcement of the mysteries
    Wherein the holy flesh is perfected,
The scourging at the pillar, and the flies
    That hum around the breast and bloody
    head.

The Passion of Love.—4. *The Harlot*

THIS day no Cyrenean stranger bore
    The Cross whereon is our Redemption
      nailed.
  But they who drove him, when at first he
    failed
Beneath it, all his limbs being wounded sore,
Found near at hand a maiden by her door,
    Whom soon they burdened; and her
      strength availed.
    But always certain clowns against her railed
And many stones her crimsoned vesture tore.

Alas, it is our kin have done this deed,
    Our chosen friends, our fathers, and our
      sons,
      With whose uncleanness our souls are
        unclean.
Have mercy, nor for thy just vengeance plead!
    By the pale brow whence still the cold
      sweat runs,
      Entreat not God against us, Magdalene!

(84)

The Passion of Love.—5. The Death of Love

O LOOK no more for his descent! No
more,
　　While the crowd threaten and the
　　　priests despise,
　Cry out upon him, but with mournful eyes
Loosen his body.　Lo now, he who bore
Our sorrows, our infirmities, and wore
　　Our weakness as a garment, now Love dies.
　　This man desires him and this man denies ;
But who of all his people shall adore ?

Call no more on him to descend ;　with myrrh
　　Anoint him, and remembering how he died
　　Keep yourselves yet for three days purified
With fasting :　watch beside his sepulchre.
　　We know not ;　surely Love may rise again,
　　Who on the cross of all men's lust was
　　　slain.

LXXVIII

The Passion of Love.—6. The Resurrection and Evangel of Love

THERE was a light about us suddenly,
　　There was a Voice commanding us,
　　　which said :
" Why seek ye still the living with the dead?
He goes before you into Galilee."
O dear land of green hills and breaking sea,
　　In our far journeys well rememberèd,
　　Thy fields once more our stumbling feet
　　　shall tread,
Our wandering ways have brought us back
　　to thee !

Love called us and we left our fathers' ships :
　　Then for three years we followed after him,
　　　Being not indolent to speak his praise,
　　　But not till the fulfilment of his days
　　Were our eyes lightened which till then
　　　were dim :
Now is his message fire upon our lips.

Of Marriage and of its Priesthood

Here shall no pagan foot nor claw of beast
    Enter ; nor wizard sorcery be seen.
    But sometime here have all true lovers been,
Nor hath the tale of outland riders ceased.
With hands of consecration now the priest
    Exalts the holy sacrament between
    The altar lights. Now, if your souls be clean,
Draw near : Himself Love gives you in His feast.

Whose voice in solemn ritual lifted up
    Praises the Name of Love ? Whose hands have blest
For you, His votaries, the mysterious Cup,
And set before you the ordained Food ?
    Voice of Himself, to narrow vows professed,
And hands of His adorable maidenhood.

LXXX

The Consummation

Now to its end draws on the bridal night :
  Now shall they reap who yesterday
    would sow,
  Nor what may be their harvest can they
    know,
Stretched on the golden couch of their
  delight :
To whom with dawn sound trumpets. From
  that height
    Whereon the spearmen watch the plains
      below
    Do these forewarn the city of what foe ?
Or hail what king returning from his fight ?

Sleep yet ! This is our holy day we greet,
  With notes of silver echoing its fame.
Sleep ! Toward white gates, down many a
  shouting street,
Masters of hope and passion and sorrow, we,
  With clash of sword on shield, move and
    acclaim
The solemn Feast of Love's Virginity.

(88)

Of Renunciation

Dıᴅsᴛ thou stretch forth thy hands, O
    queen of pain,
  And find no help, after the angel stood
  Before thee to compel thy maidenhood ?
Was thy mouth steadfast always to refrain
From grace, however the man's eyes were
    fain ?
  Love being thy need, was Faith thy
    habitude ?
  O Mary Mother, from thine own sad rood
Hush us to silence if our souls complain !

For this cause also did the Lord our God
  Abjure His love deifical, set aside
His comeliness, upon a hard path trod :
And, His Beloved so to gain, denied
  His strength, Who could have won her
    with a nod.
He hath renounced—how else to win ?—His
    Bride.

LXXXII

The Lover, ending, praises his Lady in the Fullness of Love

Lo, now I bind upon this most fair brow
   A new phylactery—if my fingers there
Lingered a little moment in the hair
Shall it not be forgiven me ?—and now
Have I accomplished the accepted vow,
   Have wrought the image that Time's
      followers bear
   Into the world's house : under it the stair
Gleams to the feet of virgin loves.   But thou,
Dear and my lady, being in presence, who
Should boast high things or labours there-
      unto ?
   How littly so small deed that so much mars!
So small ? so great ! on earth such praise of
      thee
To utter as, for sign and weaponry,
   God gave the lonely angels of the stars.